PREFACE.

THE following pages have not been hastily
written, but are the result of patient and thought-
ful research. Care has been taken that no
statement should be made without proof of its
correctness. Numerous books and records have
been consulted and untiring efforts made to
obtain the facts. One object of the writer was
to trace the lineage of the Dunbar family back
to the original progenitor, or head, and then fol-
low the line of descendants down to the present
time. The line of descendants for which he had
particular regard was that which embraced Earl
George Dunbar and Robert Dunbar.

In his research for facts that would be of
interest, the author found that the ancestors of
Earl George Dunbar extended back many genera-
tions from him, and that they for a long time had
an entirely different name. The following pages
contain the name of the original head, and also
the changes of the name and how it came to be
used as the name of a man.

It is believed that much interest will be found

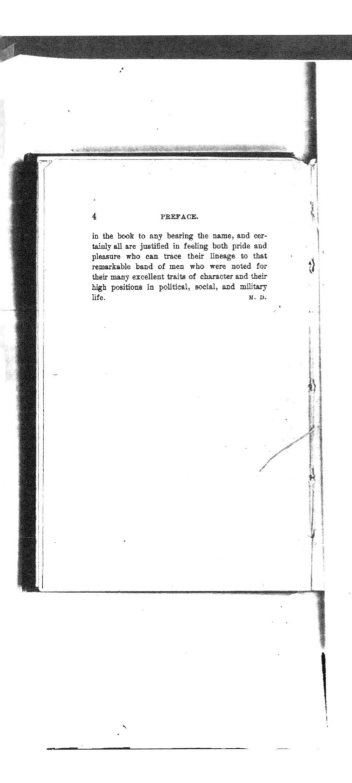

in the book to any bearing the name, and certainly all are justified in feeling both pride and pleasure who can trace their lineage to that remarkable band of men who were noted for their many excellent traits of character and their high positions in political, social, and military life. M. D.

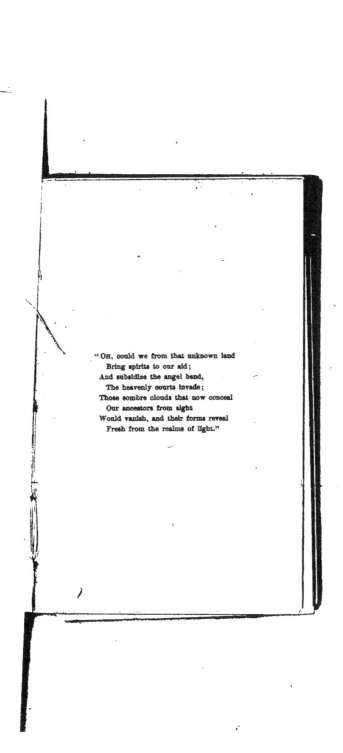

" Oh, could we from that unknown land
    Bring spirits to our aid;
And subsidize the angel band,
    The heavenly courts invade;
Those sombre clouds that now conceal
    Our ancestors from sight
Would vanish, and their forms reveal
    Fresh from the realms of light."

DUNBAR GENEALOGY.

THE name of Dunbar, or rather the last syllable, was in use more than one thousand years before the Christian era.

A historian,[1] speaking of Kennethus, says: "He drove out the Picts, distributed their lands among the soldiers, and gave many places and countries new names; and all the country from which the Picts were driven was called Fife, from an eminent person, whose name was Fifus, and Baroduma, who was so called from a great man whose name was Bar."

Although the name Dunbar appears very early in history as the name of a place, it was not used, I think, as the name of a person until after the following letter of Alexander.

ANNO 1244. — LETTER OF ALEXANDER, KING OF SCOTLAND: —

To all who shall read of the faithful, directing that, among others who shall serve with good faith and love, the King of England, is named Patrick, count of Dunbar.

[1] Burton's History of Scotland.

After this the name was applied to persons as well as places, as in the following passage: "This Earl Patrick Dunbar, after having served his king and country for some years, was influenced by the zeal of those times and engaged in the Crusades."

The Dunbar family during a period of more than three hundred years — from 1250 — occupied a very conspicuous place in the political, social, and military history of Scotland.

There were three families who held the title of Earl of March, or Merch, — Dunbar, Stewart, and Douglas.

George Dunbar II, born in 1860, at his father's death, in 1416, became tenth Earl of Dunbar and fifth Earl of March, or Merch.

This earl was much in favor with the regents during the absence of King James I, and with the king himself for several years after his return. It is about this time that he is spoken of as "possessing immense wealth." He had no sooner entered upon his fortune than he was employed as a commissioner to treat of the king's release, whereby he was liberated upon paying forty thousand pounds.

On the marriage of King James he made twenty-two knights, of whom George Dunbar was one. Hitherto this family of Dunbar had been held in the greatest favor; but this was changed about this time, for on the twelfth of March, 1425, the king at Parliament in Perth caused Earl George Dunbar to be imprisoned on suspicion. The king seized upon the Castle of Dunbar, and, having called a Parliament, caused the title of Earl George to be forfeited, confiscated his great estate and annexed it to the Crown.[2]

Camden, in his Britannica, says: "The posterity of Gospatrick, besides very large possessions in Scotland, held the barony of Bengely in Northumberland. But in the reign of King James I, George Dunbar, earl of March, by authority of Parliament and upon account of his father's rebellion, lost the proprietary and possession of the earldom of March and the seigniory of Dunbar. It was provided by the laws that the father's transgressions should succeed to the children, lest at any time, being heirs to their father's rashness as well as estate, they should, out of vain opinion of their power,

[2] Burke's Peerage.

plot against the prince and country." So notwithstanding we are regular descendants of Earl George Dunbar, who was at one time "immensely rich," we shall not fall heirs to a fortune in Scotland.

The Scots, though weakened by divisions among themselves and jealous of the prince they supported, had assembled an army with which Charles entered England; Cromwell followed, attacked, and defeated the royal troops. That battle ruined, for the time, the royal cause. The nation was now divided into many parties, and multitudes of the people had become weary of agitation and change and desired the revival of the monarchy. Fears of popery were increased by the marriage of the king with Catherine of Portugal, a Catholic princess. The condition of political affairs throughout the entire country was unsettled and afforded no promise of permanent peace.

It is not difficult to see why so many at that time inquired " if there were not in all the world a spot where there were fewer kings and wars and murders, and more peace and happiness and real prosperity; and turned their thoughts to, and sought, 'the land of the free.' "

With others, three judges — Goff, Whally,
and Dixwell — fled to New England; and it
was about this time that Robert Dunbar left
Scotland.

From the Scots' Charters and the Register
of Kelso, it appears that the Earls of Dunbar and March were descendants of Gospatrick, earl of Northumberland. After
Northumberland became a province, the
earls were only official and provincial and
not hereditary, and they were often changed
at the pleasure of the sovereign.

The most ancient histories of England and
Scotland reveal that our progenitor, or head,
lived before the conquest of England by
William, duke of Normandy.

His name was Crinan. He was born in
970, and was Saxon of Northumberland.

His son Maldred was born in 1000. This
was the Maldred who was the progenitor of
that great and honorable family of the
Nevils, of which ancient history so fre-
quently speaks.

His son Earl Gospatrick I was born in
1025. His name, in full, was Waldeve Gos-

patrick. He married the daughter and heiress of Patrick Dunbar. His family register : —

"My wife, Algithe.

"My children: Dolfin, born in Northumberland, in 1050; Waltheof, born in Northumberland, in 1055; Gospatrick, born in Northumberland, in 1060; Ethelreda, born in Northumberland, in 1065."

Earl Gospatrick II was born in Northumberland, England, in 1060, and taken into Scotland with his father in 1068, and at his father's death succeeded him as Thane of Lothean, and afterward became the first earl in Scotland.

Earl Gospatrick III, born at Dunbar, Scotland, 1100, was second Earl of Dunbar.

Earl Waldeve, born at Dunbar, Scotland, 1130, was third Earl of Dunbar.

Earl Patrick I, born in 1160, at Dunbar, Scotland, first son of Waldeve, became fourth Earl of Dunbar at his father's death in 1182.

Earl Patrick II, born 1185, at Dunbar, Scotland, first son of Patrick I, was fifth Earl of Dunbar.[1]

Earl Patrick III, born in 1210. He mar-

1 Dugdale's Baronage, published 1675.

ried Christiana, daughter of Robert Bruce, lord of Amandale, and by her had a son, born in 1235, at Dunbar, Scotland, who was Earl Patrick IV. He was the first whom we find styled Earl of March.

Earl Patrick V, born 1265, at Dunbar, Scotland, first son of Patrick V, was seventh Earl of Dunbar and second Earl of March.

Earl Patrick VI, born 1300, at Dunbar, Scotland, was eighth Earl. of Dunbar and third Earl of March.

Earl George I, born at Dunbar, Scotland, 1330, was ninth Earl of Dunbar and second Earl of Merray.

Earl and Knight George Dunbar II, born in 1360, was the tenth Earl of Dunbar and fifth Earl of March. His brother, Patrick Dunbar, "was a hostage of the king, and lived for some time at the Court of St. James. His uncle, Sir Patrick Dunbar, of Beil, was murdered with King James I, 1437."

Thus "the distinct line of the ancient and great family of Dunbar, earls of Dunbar and March, became extinct."[1]

Besides the descendants, as given in the

[1] Rebellion in Scotland.

preceding pages, there are several branches
from the parent stock that should be noticed.

And the first is, Earl of Morey; Earl
John Dunbar, who was born in 1332, at
Dunbar, Scotland. He married Lady Mar-
gery Stewart, daughter of King Robert II
of Scotland. "And that king, by his charter
of the ninth of March, 1372, gave the earldom of Morey to this John." Earl Thomas
Dunbar, son of John; Earl Thomas, son of
Thomas; Sir James Dunbar, son of Thomas;
Sir Alexander Dunbar, son of James, born
at Dunbar, Scotland, 1405. "He married
Isabel, daughter of Alexander Southerland,
of which marriage all the families of the
name of Dunbar now (1811) flourishing in
Scotland are descended."

DUNBAR, OF GRANGE HILL. — Ninian
Dunbar, born in 1575, was the founder of
the family of Dunbars, of Grange Hill.

The names of his sons were Robert, David,
and William. His descendants became quite
numerous.

DUNBAR, OF KIRK HILL. — David Dunbar was born in 1618. He settled in Kirk

.

Hill, and from him most, if not all, of the families descended.

Among his descendants are found the names of John, Rev. Robert, Rev. Sir William, who was fifth Baronet of Nova Scotia. Besides the above there have been about five hundred of his descendants whose names have passed into history.

DUNBAR, OF KINKORTH AND DURN. — Sir William Dunbar is the first named among that settlement, which became numerous. They were also very enterprising. He was born in 1615.

DUNBAR, OF HEMPRIGGS. — Born in 1750, and was the progenitor of the Dunbar family of Hempriggs and North Scotland.

His sons were Alexander, John, and William. His descendants have been very numerous, and the most of them that are now living reside at Hempriggs and North Scotland.

The last one of his descendants mentioned in history was William C. Dunbar, who was born July 20, 1844. The Dunbars of Hempriggs were the male lineal descendants of the

elder branch of the Dunbars until they failed
in Sir Patrick Dunbar, the third baronet of
their line.[1]

After that the regular line in this family
can not be reliably traced in history.

The reader will observe that, from Earl
George Dunbar, who was born in 1360, to
Robert Dunbar, who was born in 1680, —
a period of two hundred and seventy years,
— no name of any of our ancestors is
recorded in the regular line during that
time. Now it appears in the "Rebellion of
Scotland" that his uncle, Sir Patrick Dunbar,
of Beil, was murdered with King James I, in
1487, and that "the distinct line of the
ancient family of Dunbar, earls of Dunbar
and March, became extinct."

But in the account given in history of one
of the branches of the parent stock, "Dunbar, of Grange Hill," it appears that Ninian
Dunbar was born in 1575, and it is probable,
though not certain, that Robert Dunbar was
a son of Ninian Dunbar; in fact, it says he
had a son by the name of Robert.

As to the origin of the Dunbars, the regular line of descendants, and the reason for

[1] This illustrates one of the difficulties of tracing the regular
line of descendants.

the belief that Robert Dunbar was a descend-
ant of Earl George Dunbar in the regular
line, the reader, with the facts presented in
this genealogy, is as well prepared to form an
opinion as the compiler.

From the diary of Rev. Peter Hobert, the
first settled minister at Hingham, Massachusetts, 1635, it appears that Robert Dunbar,
Francis McFarland, and John Magoon came
from Scotland and settled in Hingham in
1655.

The opinion generally prevailed in Hingham that Mr. Dunbar brought money enough
with him to begin life without embarrass-
ment, as for years there were but two men
in the place who paid a higher tax.

Where he was married and what his wife's
surname was, the compiler has not been able
to ascertain.

ROBERT DUNBAR, born in Scotland, 1630;
married Rose ——. Robert died October 5,
1693. Rose died November 10, 1700.

Children: John, *b.* December 1, 1657.
Mary, *b.* October 25, 1660. Joseph, *b.* March
13, 1662. James, *b.* June 1 1664. Robert,
Jr., *b.* September 6, 1666. Peter, *b.* November 1, 1668. Joshua, *b.* October 6, 1670.

All born in Hingham, Massachusetts. Mary married Isaac Harris.

JOSHUA DUNBAR, son of Robert and Rose, married Hannah Hatch, September 21, 1699.

Children: Joshua, *b.* September 11, 1700. Benjamin, *b.* May 15, 1701. Hannah, *b.* December 12, 1703. Robert, *b.* January 16, 1705. Solomon, *b.* September 18, 1709. Stephen, *b.* October 28, 1716.

All born in Hingham.

SOLOMON DUNBAR, married Rachel Damon, of Hingham, November 23, 1738. He died in Newcastle, Maine, in 1795.

Children: Solomon, *b.* August 6, 1740. Rachel, *b.* May 22, 1742. Jesse, *b.* June 26, 1744. Olive, *b.* June 8, 1746. Lucy, *b.* July 29, 1749. Percis, *b.* November 20, 1752. Elijah, *b.* February 14, 1756.

All born in Hingham.

JESSE DUNBAR, born in Hingham, June 26, 1744; was married twice. February 11, 1762, he married Azuba Conant. She died within a few years. July 31, 1766, he married Mary Stone, of Stoughton, Massachusetts.

Jesse died in Nobleboro', Maine, in 1806. Mary died in Nobleboro', May 14, 1818.

Children: Polly, *b.* December 16, 1766. Molley, *b.* July 3, 1769. Rachel and Sarah, *b.* July 2, 1771. Persis, *b.* May 12, 1773. Lydia, *b.* February 12, 1775. Died November 2, 1775. Lydia, *b.* September 13, 1776. Mahitabel, *b.* October 5, 1778. Cate, *b.* February 27, 1780. Jesse, *b.* April 4, 1782. Olive, *b.* July 28, 1785.

JESSE DUNBAR married Sarah Winslow, of Nobleboro', Maine, December 25, 1805. Born October 1, 1787.

Sarah died August 3, 1869.

Jesse died December 8, 1872.

Children: Jesse, *b.* October 5, 1806. Sarah, *b.* October 16, 1808. Mary, *b.* October 18, 1810. Angeline, *b.* November 8, 1812. Albert, *b.* January 21, 1815. Melzar, *b.* January 10, 1817. Ursula Abigail, *b.* May 22, 1819. Newell, *b.* April 3, 1821. Dorothy Jane, *b.* December 28, 1823. Edward Winslow, *b.* April 16, 1826. Lorenzo, *b.* October 19, 1829.

All born in Nobleboro', Maine.

JESSE DUNBAR married Sarah Clark, of Nobleboro', April 15, 1828. She was born March 15, 1807.

Second marriage to Ruth Ames, of Jefferson, December 30, 1849; born July 24, 1806.

Children by first wife: Ruel Williams, *b.* December 30, 1828. Alva Sinclair, *b.* May 26, 1830. Martha Jane, *b.* February 12, 1833. Sarah Winslow, *b.* September 21, 1839.

Sarah died January 13, 1849.
Ruel W. died April 17, 1852.
Alva S. died January 2, 1857.
Jesse died October 14, 1873.

MARTHA JANE married Chauncy Addison Swift, May 25, 1851. He was born in Warren, March 26, 1817.

Children: Marilla Mason, born in Monroe, January 8, 1853. Flora Augusta, born in Rockland, January 31, 1855. Wilmont Hilton, born in Union, February 24, 1859.

MARILLA M. married Thomas Edwin Carpenter, October 21, 1876. He was born in Eastport, Maine, October 14, 1828.

Children: Alva Berton, born in Liberty,

March 9, 1878. Sarah Genella, born in Liberty, December 28, 1880.

FLORA A. married William Austin Millay, March 20, 1876. He was born in Rockland, February 27, 1850.

Children: Bertha Lola, born in Montville, March 10, 1874.

WILMONT H. married Mary Lillian Knowels, November 4, 1882. She was born in China, Maine, December 10, 1863.

SARAH W. married Lorenzo Allen Meservy, December 13, 1862. He was born in Jefferson, January 27, 1838.

Children: Ulric Day, born in Jefferson, November 29, 1866. Jesse Dunbar, born in Jefferson, December 1, 1877.

SARAH DUNBAR married Elisha Rollins Palmer, February 17, 1833. He was born in Nobleboro', June 1, 1807. Died November 10, 1868.

Children: Halsey Healey, *b.* November, 8, 1833. Arlinda Emeline, *b.* January 13, 1836. Bethena Almeda, *b.* June 5,

1838. Orlando Augustus, *b.* November, 22, 1840. Zuinglus Collins, *b.* March 22, 1843. Sarah Jane, *b.* October 10, 1845. Byron Washington, *b.* March 16, 1849, Sanford Kingsbury, *b.* March 2, 1852.

HALSEY H. married Mary Jane Maddocks, September 12, 1857. She was born July 7, 1835.

Children: Elwood Augustus, born in Nobleboro', December 18, 1859. Mary Emeline, born in Brewer, January 9, 1868.

DEATHS. — Elwood A., May 21, 1861. Halsey H., September 19, 1869. Mary Emeline, December 11, 1876.

ARLINDA EMELINE married John Leishman Clark, of Newcastle, April 25, 1856. He was born December 21, 1826.

Children: Julia Carter, *b.* November 29, 1856. Lovesta Wells, *b.* November 9, 1858. Orlando Palmer, *b.* August 12, 1860. Berthena Almeda, *b.* November 16, 1861. Sarah Palmer, *b.* April 1, 1863. John Leishman, *b.* February 23, 1866. Sophronia Maria, *b.* August 24, 1867. Orlando Augustus, *b.* July 30, 1871. Homer Caswell, *b.* November 25, 1875. All born in Newcastle, Maine.

DEATHS. — Orlando P., August 20, 1861. John L., Jr., February 23, 1886. John L., October 31, 1884.

BERTHENA A. married John Willard Chapman, of Nobleboro', June 14, 1855. He was born March 20, 1831.
Children : Edward Everett, born in Nobleboro', September 4, 1858. Sarah Emma, born in Newcastle, May 29, 1861.

EDWARD E. married Julia Evelyn Dobson, November 21, 1882; born in Jollicue, New Brunswick, July 4, 1854.

SARAH E. married David Winslow Wiswell, May 30, 1882; born in Brewer, May 9, 1858.
Children : Lillian Evelyn Wiswell, born in Boston, Massachusetts, July 13, 1888.

ZUINGLUS COLLINS married Charlotte Augusta Ware, of Brewer, December 18, 1871. She was born January 14, 1848.
Children : Nellie Goodnow, born in Brewer, September 4, 1872. Gertrude Augusta, born in Brewer, May 14, 1876. Artell Elisha,

born in Brewer, February 2, 1878. Flora Elizabeth, born in Brewer, September 12, 1883.

SARAH JANE married David Davis Tarr, born in Salem, Maine, May 2, 1839. Married September 16, 1880.

Children: Arthur Jay, *b.* June 18, 1882. Alta May, *b.* June 18, 1882.

BYRON W. married Etta May Jordan, December 25, 1875. She was born in Maria-ville, June 22, 1850.

Children: Maud Josephine, *b.* June 25, 1877. Halsey Edward, *b.* March 19, 1880. Died in 1880. Jessie Berthena, *b.* January 21, 1882.

SANFORD R. married Eva Augusta Tibbetts, November 30, 1876. She was born in Brewer, August 12, 1852.

Children: Fred Sanford, *b.* July 11, 1877. Ada Baker, *b.* September 11, 1879. Hazel Augusta, *b.* August 13, 1882.

MARY DUNBAR married Daniel Moody, of Nobleboro', in 1834. He was born December 30, 1811.

Children: Ann Medora, born in Thomaston, September 12, 1885. Kendall Washburn, born in Thomaston, July 1, 1887. Mary Adelaide, born in Thomaston, January 12, 1846. Adelbert Dunbar, born in Thomaston, August 2, 1849. Kendall W. died June 6, 1855.

ANN MEDORA married Joseph Edward Catland, of Thomaston, October 17, 1857. He was born August 11, 1836.

Children: Osgood Smith, born in Thomaston, December 23, 1859. Carrie Amelia, born in Thomaston, December 6, 1861. Edward Kendall, born in Thomaston, November 9, 1865.

OSGOOD S. married Aurelia A. Dunning, of Moore's Flat, Nevada County, California, April 6, 1883. She was born September 28, 1861.

CARRIE A. married Charles Edward Hastings, of Union, June 3, 1882. He was born December 8, 1855.

Children: Ella May, born in Thomaston, March 29, 1883.

MARY ADELAIDE married Harrison Emery, of South Thomaston, October 16, 1876. He was born in South Thomaston, April 30, 1841.

ADELBERT D. married Issa Dora Kent, of Brewer, October 10, 1874. She was born November 21, 1854.

Children: Kendall Osgood, born in Thomaston, July 4, 1876. Died September 4, 1876. Issa Dora died in Thomaston, July 16, 1876. Adelbert's second wife was Nettie Medbury, of Lynn, Massachusetts, born February 24, 1852; married September 26, 1880.

Children: Alice May, born in Lynn, Massachusetts, August 27, 1881.

ANGELINE DUNBAR married Lot Chapman, of Nobleboro', July 6, 1850. He was born August 10, 1813.

Children: Annie Angeline, born in Nobleboro', August 17, 1856. Died September 15, 1865. Lot died December 25, 1880.

ALBERT DUNBAR married Elizabeth Talbot Rich, of Hope, June 21, 1842. She was born January 31, 1821.

Children : Albert Wayland, born in Knox, June 17, 1843. Judson Boardman, born in Patten, July 6, 1848. Lizzie, born in Freedom, October 12, 1850. Alice, born in Alfred, August 12, 1857.

JUDSON B. married Ella Caroline Clark, of Fairfield, Maine, May 10, 1871. She was born February 19, 1848.

Children : Robert Wayland, born in Portland, Maine, January 24, 1872. Mary Elizabeth, born in Portland, Maine, October 18, 1873. Philip, born in Portland, Maine, December 1, 1877.

ALICE married Rev. Sumner Abram Ives, September 19, 1881; born in Suffield, Connecticut, 1842.

Children : Sumner Albert, born in Alfred, July 23, 1882.

MELZAR DUNBAR married Minerva Hopkins, of Jefferson, Maine, December 15, 1842. She was born June 21, 1822.

Children : Euzilla Minerva, born in Hope, Maine, January 1, 1844. Clara Prescott, born in Albion, Maine, December 15, 1845.

Eugene Kincaid, born in Albion, Maine, October 11, 1847. Melzar Preston, born in Monroe, Maine, November 19, 1849. Lucy Thatcher, born in Monroe, Maine, January 28, 1854. Ella Maria, born in Surrey, Maine, September 17, 1856. John Bickmore, born in St. George, Maine, October 20, 1864.

EUZILLA M. married Calvin Leach, of Penobscot, Maine, October 10, 1862. He was born January 7, 1885.
Children: Eugene Calvin, born in Penobscot, Maine, November 18, 1863. Albert Preston, born in Penobscot, Maine, November 8, 1868.

CLARA P. married James Hiram Davis, of St. George, Maine, November 26, 1865. He was born January 28, 1888.
Children: Herbert Harris, born in St. George, Maine, April 25, 1867. Louisa Bliss, born in St. George, Maine, July 5, 1869. Nellie Lucy, born in St. George, Maine, July 20, 1875.
Louisa B. died March 10, 1875.

EUGENE KINCAID married Janette Everett Richardson, of North Attleboro', Massachusetts, December 9, 1875. She was born September 19, 1845.

Children: Stephen Richardson, born in North Attleboro', Massachusetts, November 14, 1876. Eugene Melzar, born in North Attleboro', Massachusetts, July 24, 1878. Florence Janette, born in Boston, Massachusetts, September 14, 1880.

MELZAR P. married Marietta Chase Snow, of Brooklyn, New York, August 26, 1875. She was born in Brunswick, Maine, October 18, 1856.

Children: Nettie May, born in New Haven, Connecticut, March 5, 1877. Robert Bruce, born in New Haven, Connecticut, October 5, 1882.

Robert B. died July 23, 1884.

LUCY T. married Peables Patrick Robinson, of St. George, Maine, October 7, 1878. He was born in Warren, Maine, August 6, 1833. Died in St. George, Maine, September, 5, 1879.

Children: Gertrude Minerva, born in

Camden, Maine, February 22, 1879. Died
in Penobscot, Maine, October 18, 1880.

ELLA MARIA married Charles H. Kidder,
of Richmond, Maine. May 18, 1878. He was
born in Dresden, Maine, November 9, 1847.
   Children: William Hopkins Kidder, born
in Callao Bay, on the American ship *James-
town*, May 10, 1879. Grace Browning, born
in Richmond, Maine, June 26, 1880. Charles
Hogan, born in Richmond, Maine, February
20, 1882.

URSULA ABIGAIL married James Sulli-
van Trask, of Jefferson, Maine, September
24, 1842. He was born April 3, 1817.
   Children: Evander Sullivan, born in New
Hampton, New Hampshire, May 13, 1845.
Paulena Ursula. born in Nobleboro', Maine,
May 14, 1847.   Lorena Abigail, born in
Nobleboro', Maine, May 27. 1850. James
Newall. born in Nobleboro', Maine, August
18. 1852. Albert Spurgeon, born in Noble-
boro', Maine. April 19, 1859. Judson Has-
seltine, born in Nobleboro', Maine, February
16. 1861.
   DEATHS. — Paulena U., August 28, 1848.

Ursula A., April 27, 1876. Judson H., January 4, 1882.

LORENA A. married Edward Tappan Hodge, of Edgecomb, Maine, September 19, 1867. He was born March 10, 1844.

Children: Willie Edward, born in Edgecomb, Maine, July 15, 1868. Abbie Tappan, born in Edgecomb, Maine, August 18, 1869.

Willie E. died August 22, 1868.

JAMES NEWELL married Mary Norton, of Portland, Oregon, April 21, 1877. She was born February 2, 1862.

Children: Clarence Newell, born in Silver City, Idaho, September 16, 1878. James Francis, born in Silver City, May 18, 1880. Maud Ursula, born in Silver City, November 6, 1882.

Mary N. died May 23, 1884.

EVANDER S. married Nettie Clarinda Hopkins, of Jefferson, Maine, February 25, 1875. She was born November 16, 1845.

Children: Ira Hopkins, born in Nobleboro', December 17, 1879. Florence Judson, born in Nobleboro', April 25, 1883.

ALBERT S. married Clara Hodgkins Chapman, June 16, 1879. She was born in Jefferson, Maine, December 22, 1861.

NEWELL DUNBAR, died April 14, 1842, at the age of 21 years, 11 days.

DOROTHY JANE DUNBAR married John Weeks Perkins, November 4, 1852. He was born in Nobleboro', Maine, January 31, 1825.
Children: John Alston, born in Nobleboro', Maine, December 28, 1853. Lorenzo Dunbar, born in Nobleboro', Maine, February 12, 1855. Estella Jane, born in Nobleboro', Maine, November 26, 1857.

JOHN ALSTON married Lizzie Sarah Pilsbury, December 8, 1877. She was born in Nobleboro', July 13, 1853.
Children: Bessie Estella, born in Nobleboro', Maine, December 28, 1880. Georgie Phebe, born in Nobleboro', July 13, 1882.

LORENZO D. married Georgianna Augusta Candage, June 4, 1888. She was born at Bluehill, Maine, August 16, 1852.

ESTELLA JANE married Lyman E. Winslow, of Nobleboro', January 28, 18 5.

EDWARD W. DUNBAR married Lucinda Pool Burnham, of Edgecomb, Maine, November 4, 1852. She was born June 13, 1830.
Children: Edward Everett, born in Nobleboro, January 13, 1854. Lizzie Lucinda, born in Nobleboro', November 24, 1855. Kendall Moody, born in Nobleboro', September 18, 1857. Willis Burnham, born in Nobleboro', February 25, 1860. Herbert Allen, born in Nobleboro', March 22, 1862. Hattie Winslow, born in Newcastle, September 7, 1864. Merton Webster, born in Newcastle, November 7, 1867.

EDWARD E. married Mary Annie Day, of Damariscotta, Maine, November 22, 1876. She was born September 8, 1854.
Children: Mabel Annie, born in Damariscotta, January 18, 1878. Harold Everett, born in Damariscotta, December 10, 1879. Alice Lucinda, born in Damariscotta, March 13, 1883.

KENDALL M. DUNBAR married Laura Estella Castner, of Damariscotta, June 27, 1885.

HERBERT ALLEN DUNBAR married Mary Estell Clark, of Damariscotta, December 10, 1884.
Children: Mary Palmer Dunbar, *b.* October 2, 1885.

LORENZO DUNBAR married Angeletta Hall, of Nobleboro', June 18, 1856. She was born May 13, 1837.
Children: Ella Jane, *b.* January 17, 1857. Edson Lorenzo, *b.* July 15, 1859. Sarah Abbie, *b.* March 7, 1862. Angie Maria, *b.* March 20, 1864. Gustena, *b.* August 25, 1866.
Angeletta died June 12, 1870. Ella Jane died March 1, 1875.
Second marriage to Sarah Hall, of Nobleboro', July 3, 1873. She was born August 2, 1839.
Children: Lettie Maud, *b.* March 24, 1874. Linda Alice, *b.* October 18, 1875. Lester Albert, *b.* October 18, 1875.

SARAH A. married Frank Leslie Welt, of

Waldoboro', Maine, September 4, 1884. He
was born in Waldoboro', September 4, 1859.
Children: Howard Lorenzo Welt, born in
Waldoboro', Maine, October 11, 1885.